a shape that is wet
and slippery...

Jenny's paddling pool.
It's round.

What other round things can you see?

I
spy
with my
little eye

a shape that you can build with...

Luke's building blocks. They are square.

What other squares can you see?

I
spy
with my
little eye

a shape that flutters
in the breeze...

the sails
on Ben's
boat. They
are triangles.

What other triangles can you see?

I
spy
with my
little eye

a shape that is fun to play with...

Milly's
playmat.
It's a
rectangle.

What other rectangles can you see?

I
spy
with my
little eye

a shape that sparkles
and shines...

Sarah's cake.
It's a star.

What other stars can you see?